Riverine

Eleanor Rees

Gatehouse Press

Published by
Gatehouse Press Limited
90 Earlham Road
Norwich NR2 3HA
www.gatehousepress.com

Copyright lies with Eleanor Rees

All rights reserved. No part of this publication may be reproduced, stored in a retrieval system, or transmitted in any form or by any means, electronic, mechanical, photocopying, recording or otherwise, without the prior permission of the publishers.

This publication is sold subject to the condition that it shall not, by way of trade or otherwise, be lent, re-sold, hired out or otherwise circulated without the publisher's prior consent in any form of binding or cover other than that in which it is published and without a similar condition including this condition being imposed on the subsequent purchaser.

ISBN 978-0-9928573-8-7

About the *Lighthouse* PAMPHLETS

Lighthouse is an award-winning quarterly journal from Gatehouse Press; the *Lighthouse* pamphlets series aims to give a platform to new writers who have come to prominence in the journal and elsewhere. All staff are volunteers, and all profits go back into publishing. For more information, including how to submit work, see our website: http://www.gatehousepress.com/lighthouse/

The typefaces used in this book, IM Fell English and IM Fell DW Pica, were produced by Igino Marini and are reproduced with his kind permission: http://iginomarini.com

The Lighthouse image was designed and printed using lino cut techniques by Gini Hanbury: http://ginihanbury.blogspot.co.uk

Special thanks to Lee Seaman, James Higham and Natty Peterkin

Cover/title illustrations by Natty Peterkin, nattypeterkin.tumblr.com
Cover design by Norwich Designer
Printed and bound in the UK

Riverine

Eleanor Rees

Contents

Author's Preface   5

Drift   12
Protean Shifts   13
Suburban Epic   16
Nocturne for the Last Bus Home   17
In My Ears and In My Eyes   18
Errant   20
Seafog   21
Inside the Cloud   22
On Time   23
One Note   24
The House of the Dark Woods   26
Moon Struck   27
For You in the Half-Light   30
Congleton Tapestry   31
Mossley Hill   33
The Goat's Field   34
High Tide   36
And the Spring Said   37
St. Dynfog's Well   38
At Gob Cave   39
At Pen Môn   41
At Sea   44

Acknowledgements   46

Gatehouse Press

Preface

Many of the poems in this selection live in the locale around my home in the south of Liverpool, poems in which I am asking for a connection with a landscape supposedly mundane – the suburban road, the back yard and beyond to the cutting where the trains run by. I understand all of these poems as 'local' – that is, made from interaction with limits of season and place. The Mersey's high tide ebbs a mile from my house, trains stream behind the garden wall, beech leaves shift, geese fly, my neighbours lock the front door as they leave our flats. The 80A bus passes over the bridge though I can only hear it. Dew settles. Carbon clogs up the sky. These transitions define reality. There is no stillness and there is no lack: each local movement has an impact on the other. And poetry is another of these transitions, dynamic – a charge, a movement of energy from one state to another via rhetoric and rhythm – then travelling back out again to the interior of the reader or dispersed amongst an audience as sound and visualisation. In a world which is perpetually changing – in which there are no fixed states – the poet's work is to morph the forms we think with.

A poet's being is their material, a clay that's shaped through imagination into a vessel, a container of energy. The poet shares this shape around, passing the cup amongst the crowd. Everyone needs more or less water. No one needs the same amount. The poet must create work that can carry enough meaning to meet all these needs: so there is enough to go around. Dispersal is the communal function of the poet's work. Even a lyric is a communal form; in one way or another, everyone identifies with an 'I'.

Without connection our art-form becomes meaningless, since meaning-making is an act of alteration. The poet speaks with the river or the sea but she also continues this meaning-making process as she expands through language into her audience. Maybe, then, the audience for poetry should be thought of more as participants — joining in with the co-creation of meaning which is reading and interpretation. In my thinking and writing about poetry I use the term 'local poet' to describe these dynamic interactions: the poem becomes a collective reimagining.

Working with other people to write the poems rebuilds the connection between poet and audience. If the poet understands that they are part of dynamic systems in a living world, part of natural and social processes, then we can understand that these interactions produce the poem. The poet is the connector and maker, the joiner-together of parts to create further structures which rest in turn on the processes below. But like any natural structure, poetry can bend in the wind or be subject to erosion. Sense is not static but alterable, changing shape almost as soon as it is made. Working with processes involves imagining spatially, drawing on the varied tensions and energies that inhere in the local context, noticing them, retelling and interacting with their intentions. In the non-textual world, local context can offer form, a shape to work with that the poet can then re-form: again, the clay becomes the pot becomes clay. In the push and pull of my negotiations with reality the poems emerge, alive, hoping you will remake them, in love and in time.

*

What is the form that holds us? This is the space of the imagination, a common ground, a meeting place under the sky where we see and hear within all directions. The language of poetry — concrete, precise, resonant, metaphoric — opens out the land before us, like looking at a slope leading down to the sea. In the space created by poetic language we meet and we join, thinking differently, hypnotically, not with our critical minds but with our visual, spatial faculties. We are less enmeshed in 'my' perspective and more involved in the communal world-making of the poem. We are extended. This is an experience intangible but very real.

How we bring others into this space — not to disrupt or alienate but to include, but to transform ourselves a little, give our boundaries a stretch, roll them out and share the listening and the remaking — this is the work of poesis, the art of making.

Remembering the etymological roots for the name 'poet' returns the sense of change to the word, poetry as verb not noun, of dynamic moment when one thing becomes another. Our bodies alter moment to moment: thinking in tune with these shifts is a starting point for the local poet, sensed and situated deep inside reality and all its goings-on; speaking the changes is the challenge of the poem. In the lyric, verbs animate these moments in the self; another technique is to allow an energetic movement to emerge as music via the rhythm, harmony, narrative. Yet the narrative is not there to provide order — an explanation of events — but is a sequencing of elements for the pleasure of arranging time, long and short, fast and slow, up and down, in and out.

In a public context, such as writing to commission, the various pulls and pushes of the place and the people involved provide further structuring possibilities. What is the deadline? Who are the audience? Do they even like poetry? Often my poems emerge from projects in real places: 'Congleton Tapestry' was commissioned for a reading at Congleton Central Library in 2012, 'Mossley Hill' emerged from involvement with an academic research project on local food production in Liverpool; 'In Their Ears and In Their Eyes' is the result of an online collaboration about place, 'Protean Shifts' was written for performance on a barge; 'The Goat's Field' was written in a goat's field at the Centre for Alternative Technology, 'High Tide' is a song lyric written for folk singer Emily Portman.

Poetic form is not just patterns made with words but also the patterns made by people living in real places; it is like water threading through sand. The local poet always writes *with* the patterns she finds in the world. She takes them and reshapes them into something different: whatever is *now* required. These negotiations mean poems are produced which are fluvial: pushed and pulled out of the flows of the real into standing pools, temporal wells. By reinterpretation – listening and reading – the energy is released once more, pushing through the culverts in the culture into new shapes in someone else's life – a picture, a song, a fresh thought on the circumstances of the problem, a different mood than earlier in the day – brighter maybe, but more resonant and alive. This is how I experience good poetry, and it is what I hope to make for others, forms that can expand into other shapes and sense through the portal of the poem. In collaboration with other artists this process is intensified as the other voice or art-form offers further boundaries with which to negotiate, from which to make new outlines. The collaborative poem is that which can only be made by the dynamics of those people, in those circumstances, at that point in time.

And time is important to the local poet. It is the element which might run out. It must be ridden well, like a nervous horse, gently and with grace. Not too fast, not too slow; temporal concerns define all relational creative work. The flows and movement will be at different speeds – the project reading is on Monday, the artist needs the text by today, there is paperwork, o so much paperwork, the rain won't stop but the trains still pour through, blackbirds shrill, geese fly south, carriages with horses line the street in 1900, the first steam trains roll by, steam in the cutting, past and future become entwined, which is first and which is second we do not know.
Like stars flung across space from all angles
          the local poet catches a glimpse of bright tails
                    lighting the night sky as gas burns out to black.

Riverine

Drift

I say nothing to the night
or to the blackening folds of the cloud.
Terraced roofs are a pack of cards,
are my dream-talk of tented villages,
nomadic peoples, suburbs on the move
into the deep black sea over the coast;
long rhythms butt
against the vision inside my eye.

A house sits on a promontory
jutting into the ocean, waves at the door.
I build a wall upon its landscaped lawn
as the light falls, darkening
the dry stone and the planted border.
A black printed ink across the horizon.

Protean Shifts

I am digging me. I am swollen spore
        swum in the slow tide south
    towards the shore, dredged from
            the wildflower of the Thameside.
I form on the skin of bent-double men,
    unearthing the hollow of me,
            pick-axing mud in a spring storm
which does not stick but slides
            into their lungs. They breathe me
home to their wives, into mud,
                children born of the canal-side.

Barges' red-flowered painted swirls
like the lick of a tongue
around a glass of clean water.
I want to go outside but I
can't go any faster.

I am digging me. I am swollen spore
    like a gull at sea on and under
            to the black water bubble of the navvies'
continual thrusting cut at the rock
        in the sharp heat of endless summer,
their sweat like stars on a shoulder's shift
           from pick to impact; I stick
to the pelts of mud they wash later,
              whiskey on their lips.
On the quick route home, a young man
          splashes canal suds over his bloodshot eyes.

Barges' red-flowered painted swirls
like the lick of a tongue
around a glass of clean water.
I want to go outside but I
can't go any faster.

I am poured. I am moored. I am run.
    I glimpse in the shallow loam, a rat
        sculling its way through the parallel bricks
lined with moss and mud. Down under
    a coin punched into the sludge
        sparks as the barge's bow
    glides over like a seal's belly in far waters
    O marine radar. O transatlantic passage.
    O epic journey across the Atlantic.
Where is my north,
            my tidal surge?

Barges' red-flowered painted swirls
like the lick of a tongue
around a glass of clean water.
I want to go outside but I
can't go any faster.

I will never know you, glacial melt,
    felted as I am in earth. I settle lower
        into the legacy of dirt, appliquéd onto midlands'
  green, afternoon teas, farmyard's midden,
      and country fetes. A vicar with ruby cheeks
    walks towards me offering his hand.
    I smooth my line towards industry,
        riverine estuaries, coal-dust, turbines.

Barges' red-flowered painted swirls
like the lick of a tongue
around a glass of clean water.
I want to go outside but I
can't go any faster.

I am digging me. I am swollen spore
    flooded across the un-drained fields,
        stagnant water in molten pools, a roof far gone.
I return along roots of the beech wood copse
      through thick mud and rotten crops
until I swell overblown and ripening
      through the sluice, into the lock
        where a small child swims ragged-faced
and long-gone drowned, his skin
      like a fish's gills breathes for him as he dives.
I know him in me. I feel each final gasp.

Barges' red-flowered painted swirls
like the lick of a tongue
around a glass of clean water.
I want to go outside but I can't go any faster.

Suburban Epic

The red-eyed man has a face which flies north, peels
off his skull like bats' wings or folded paper caught
on the rain-driven wind from the sea. His eyes
gleam through the sockets, he smiles like a song,
leans on the gate outside the tight-lipped house;
bare arms on tarnished metal seep up the dew.
He waits. I walk towards him from the front door,
but falling back into buddleia at the edge of the road,
inside its willow basket I am encased in hands
which rub me like a child in a newly run bath or a grave,
and I plummet until upright and the red-eyed man stands
again at the gate, now with a face. He takes my hand
and we run like missiles through the dawn-raided side streets,
curtains buttoned down, all eyelids light on retina,
to the track into the woods, the bridle-path to nowhere,
and he purrs beneath his breath as we mate,
him behind, me on my knees. Blood spots the parkland.
Up against a tree bark swallows us, crisps over our pulse,
forms our breath, him in me. We are coppiced.
Day comes, he vanishes; we are two branches.

Nocturne for the Last Bus Home

City, before dark comes I want to sing for you, name
all net-curtained windows one by one.

All your lights turned on for an evening meal.
I want to speak your bevelled iron gates, the ring road

in full voice: a spring evening and I am full of you.
You give me whole numbers: 'up since four,' says

the woman getting on, as the bitter air breaks us
on the top deck, to the hilltop, through Fiveways on the ride

to the hospital car-park, past contracted breaths, sharp pulses,
a couple happening in the folds of your alleyways,

or the rip of skin in the maternity ward,
or on to Knotty Ash: a dragon on the playing field.

O crumbling darkness, come now come, to the blue glow
of TVs in a back room pushing across the perimeter of parkland,

patient trees in gardens waiting for someone, an ambulance
paused at the junction. The bus stops. A man,

red scarf at the neck like a wound, steps on and shadows follow
from the spooling back streets falling somewhere beneath the wheels;

wooden signposts point to cycle tracks across side roads and on
into deep quickening dusk, rushed love comes in a twilit bed,

a child's eyes spark in the floodlit sports ground and cars circle
the flower-topped roundabout while our old bus warms and hums.

In My Ears and In My Eyes

The water curves over the railway bridge
    like a cat jumping a fence, road
        laid over the thrust of the key
stone's force, and rocks
        in tumult, stepped into the space,
held for years gone past now,
pour down to the laundrette by the junction,
        where wet cotton churns in metal drums,
        sodden and soapy as an old man
sleeps in the corner: his dreaming mind
    sees circular flights
        of birds across a purple sky.
He opens his eyes; clouds reflect on his pupils.
In the window frame a centipede
    crawls along the grain
        of rotten wood through flecks
        of bright blue paint as a car parks
outside the newsagents, a narrow boat between lock gates;
    the ripples loosen the swell by the pub,
        tributaries pulse out towards the sea,
        children on the way home from school,
knee length socks and tiny rucksacks, are ships
in the wind, sail-cloth ponytails
        flapping in the bright salt-ridden sun.
    A pigeon flashes past a windscreen mirror,
        and over to the sports field behind the sandstone wall;
        soil wraps itself in green and brown,
turf billowing up and over pools of last night's
    rain. A woman
steps up from under the mud
covered with sludge; she sprints towards the gate,

        towards the lights, wet fabric clings to her form,
          and the puddle erupts. A fountain
of dirt runs as lava across this spring afternoon
and into the pub, morphing around the bar stools' legs,
layering earth and worms on the patterned carpet.
On a shelf above the bar, wine glasses rattle a shimmy,
pedestrians climb up onto garden walls to escape the tide
               and all stare back along the lane
                  as the flood drains, and beneath the remains
       are clay and brick, a supporting cast of mineral elements,
              a couple holding hands,
their blood weight of bodies walking home,
      liquid held in tension at the fold of the bones.

Errant

Or I need to live more slowly and close
to *things* — as intimate as I can
with the body of the world.

When it takes me I am reluctant,
woven into its light, I hold on:

you come, earth, on your own terms
and leave me wanting
to settle in you but you keep moving —

my neighbours leave the house,
another arrives carrying a book,
the trains in the cutting reel past,
images on film in an old camera.
A hammer verbs on a fence beyond.

All seeps towards the next hour:
turn of the moon, sun behind the cloud.

Listen: broken stream,
a drip of water in caverns beneath the hill
sounds out amongst the curtained windows.

Seafog

I run to the rain's edge, forgotten
   in the field of drizzle.
       You stood naked
  under the dying tree,
        smiling at me.
The grey encloses us, both without care,
   running down the back roads towards the city's
      ever-lasting light;
        your body unreachable,
solitary without a gift, broadening
         at the edge of the storm into a cliff face,
       your chest the height of an island cove.

I cannot climb to you though the wind is high.
The road is a slip-stream. I am shivering,
   goose-bumped and reddened, cloth-less
      and un-swaddled in a mist, sitting in
a rowing boat, long red hair streaming behind,
      rowing away, elbows cocked,
        hot breath,
   a slight sweat, nipples alert
   in the cold night.

I can not land where you are not.
I can not bring the boat to land,

to daylight, rain, wet fog, always here.

Inside the Cloud

Violet-scented, sweet colour, green voile lace leaf,
daisy whites in the short grass soaked with thundered air.

Three yellow flowers bright to the brown bark;
an iris flower open almost too far, blue petals bent back,

strata on white, stamen-yellow sticky contains a small sea of rain.
Meadow grass shaped like droplets in the wave of cornflower.

An earth path edged with red bricks reeks of mineral and mulch.
I scratch my boots along exposed soil. I am touching a scar.

I do it again; crushed sods separate beneath the leather.
Swallows turn and loop, wind their pattern over the slope.

A wet rope of black trees swings on the distance
and on the road beyond, crystalline light set in tarmac:

onyx, jet, diamonds, sparkle as the shower
reaches to thunder in from the sea behind the mountains.

I want the rain to start. I want to taste the grit of things.
The path back over the field springs up to meet each footstep.

On Time

Take me to the distance,
the hedgerow green then raw pink —

to the horizon where I can rest away from myself,
cushioned by the edge of the day's heat.

Streetlights are coming on.
Halogen spots expand perimeters in delivery yards

and the last stretch of the sun
catches the drag of the train's

determination, late for the next station;
for I become

immersed in the flood of the orange glow containing Wigan.

And when the guard announces the next stop
I am without myself,
        lost,
                somewhere behind,
                              outside the rush

in the black-red strata of the evening sky,
in a lava flow scorching country lanes,

in the motorway's fold at the junction
forming a glacial cooling tower, precipice white.

One Note

Upstairs my neighbours are singing again,

playing guitar, opening sound to the wind;
the window ajar, rooftops outside lighting

with flecks of voice, brightening
the damp tarmacked alleyway to the bridge,

the fresh fall of leaf, the old school:
a lamp clicks on in an attic room at night;

drums and piano patterning the eaves.
Wet rhythms crumbling through the decades

as cars change colour, or
the newspaper print freshens to new ink:

a child with my eyes
runs across the headland beyond this river

over the ridge to the bus stop at the precinct.
Early morning, she sings open-mouthed

to the sun as it rises along the Welsh hills,
school a dry sentence: the mountains

praised with a loose tune,
a singular love she attaches to the dawn,

to Duck Pond Lane beside the supermarket,
the small brook, dark freckles of light

where the branches reach over the path, always
the risk of silence from behind the trees,

from the shadows which precede the song,
as she flies over wet grass towards the sun.

The House of the Dark Woods

In the hollow underneath the ridge
the house is resting in the mulch
within the far dark gleam of stars.

The house seems to blink — an agony
of hours passes. It uncurls.

The windows swing like lanterns
as it rises, full-bodied and feral,
arching into a curve that blocks out the moon,

limbers forwards like startled hare
or a mountain speeded up through time.
The downstairs windows are deep sea pearls.

The glimmer of its lurching stride
lingers in the dark that follows
into the woodland dell, so craggy and alone.

The branches bend to see the house
bound panther-like into the forest
where the trees are silent and don't sway —

into the compress of bark and twig,
into the depth of the night where all is black.

Two children smile back from behind the glass,
wave like long lost relatives
sinking into the weight of the darkness.

The lights burning out; the stars fade.
The house swishes its tail and is gone.

Moon Struck

The air isn't moving today. It is quiet air:
a field of un-mown grass before a storm.

There is a child there. She is singing
as a full moon rises over the hedgerow,

opaque and yellow-singed globe
of rich rock, pawing the earth,

casting a thick shadow across the elderflower.
Child, you run like the earth turns,

you pound like a dynamo on this crusty surface,
your bare feet smashing onto crystals under-toe.

You shatter the solid matter
with each compression.

Forthright child, love this moon.
It breaks and spins into the dusk with you,

in your burning; tears, pulse, hunger.
Earthbound, ensconced in limits,

you camp under the height of the stars
for a few days which become years

and the turning grinds light to dust
you breathe into your sight,

running in a thrust of sleep
across an empty lake, the water

evaporated, your hillside campsite a border
crossing. Child, I am all for you,

but you run into the dryness, and under it;
the valley walls muster strength, rock strata

creaking into life, a virus speeds across the country,
or your lover leaves or dies or grows old,

and like the forking tongues of divining
rods the path bifurcates, a light

shines violently onto one end, a waterfall
crushes lichen at another, the space

behind you folding into and onto itself
in permanent avalanche or lava flow,

your campsite under red rock now,
the heat is a pressure as is the sky

and the sound of many voices on the horizon:
they shout 'run to the left child

run to the right'; an owl sweeps into view,
'go under' he says, 'go under', so you crawl

into the bracken stacked against the menhir
on the moor and into full-moon-time pooled

at its core and you can swim in that steam,
in cold air child, in the space between child,

in the interplay child, in the icy bowl of the other space child,

and above tectonic plates crush down the granite
and the owl screeches over the cattle in the field
and the old city in the far north is flung higher,

pelted out towards the sea, landing
rearranged, child.

Shift, O matter shift.

For You in the Half-Light

Each space I stand in with you
is soluble as salt in the sea.
The light seeps out, flees
as something else speaks in.

I can hear songs from many days away on the wind
and the familiar rush of time changing shape
in the country darkness
lit by one street lamp
and moon-bitten gaps in the hedge.

Our way is a smooth pool of open sky
fallen between earth and heavens,
edgeless and drawn out by eyes
dusted with night.
We cannot see the distances.
I hear histories spiralling into this new occasion.

Over the horizon, through the resting seaside town,
barnacles' soft bodies
encased in shell
sleep sound in their own special dark.

Congleton Tapestry

Congleton rare, Congleton rare,
Sold the Town Bible to buy a new bear.

A wedding dress weeps as a fiancé sprints away,
top hat bounding the hairline of the hedge;
and through a well-stitched corbelled window,
wide open on the kitchen table, the 1912 Chronicle documents:
'Alleged Breach of Promise in Chester Assizes'
He said they had never walked about the fields together.
He had not met to bring her home from church.
Together the town tuts and cries, then sighs.
And when quietness settles in the lanes,
more flaxen rain. On the High Street
emptiness purrs in the closed-up café
as Anglo-Saxon villagers brew a pot of broth in Priesty Fields
where houses are raised then fall again
like a screen on pause; and as they wait for the decision
of the committee, a line of concerned faces,
warm-hatted, well-booted, peep from behind the hedge,
lever a large wooden wedge which tips the land like a ship at sea.
Towards Astbury Mere a union jack slinks up a flag pole.
A woman in a terraced street tries to wedge new roller blinds in her car boot.
In a window box a ginger cat strokes a spider with his arching tail.
And somewhere in 1600 a bear rushes through the shopping precinct
pursued by revellers. He expands in the damp Cheshire air,
and a waterfall of rain pours from his giant's fur,
which turns the looms in the factories by the river Dane,
fustian cut to velvet feathers the street with down,
until wet nose at the height of the burial cairn,
the bear slows and bites the edge of the rock,
sharp teeth shaping out the ridge, then turns

and pulses, vanishing into the dusk
where below on the plain, beyond the viaduct, observatory
telescope at an angle to the night like an eye,
the land begins to quake, rock strata
jolt and shake old earth into lucent hills,
rolling slope, glacial lakes. The future waits.

Mossley Hill

On the footbridge lads meet to smoke
with their eyes closed; trains pummel underneath
and beyond them blue summer sky is streaked pink:
fresh wind from the Mersey rustles their shirts.
Down the road in the Chinese a man waits for his order,
the old lady serving speaks in bright Cantonese
and along the alley outside the take-away window
the back-to-backs are face-to-face,
hanging baskets topping in the breeze;
and in my eye-line from the counter to the back of the pub,
lamps flick on in the side bar, footie on the TV,
lovers under the pergola. A couple walk in:
she has pillar-box lips; two lads drink frothy pints
at an iron-legged table, one thumbs a roll-up,
steps outside to savour it as the late sun
rolls across the curve of the hill while
in the allotments at the back of the semis
a man raises a fork which glints as the moon
swollen and ripe, peckers the treetops,
dry mouth folding onto tips of the leaves:
and on the ridge, near the big house, a fire sparks in the woods,
an iron-age hill fort rises from the mulch,
menhir in their padlocked greenhouse
carve spiral patterns onto damp cold rock,
cows ache for the dairy, in the piggery sows give birth;
in the orchard behind the stable-yard
an apple falls to the floor, a child grabs it, runs through a wall
and away into the station where the first trains ran.
A man lies on the track, on blood-sodden gravel,
guard pale-faced, hands cupped around his eyes.
An ambulance soars over the hump of the bridge
like a halo of light; too late tonight,
and in the hedgerow mice seep into shadow,
scramble through fencing; a cat sleeps on the far wall.

The Goat's Field

A cockerel scratches a cry into the afternoon.
Bright sun whites its eyes
on corrugated tin.

Voltaic panels grasp the heat along the roofs
                  of huddled dwellings –

four geese take-off up the field,
orange feet capping the tops of the long grass,
then settle back to shadows
as if there's no need to startle;
waddle along their desire-track towards the
                              small holding –

a cricket taps, corn-flowers lilt,
a spiral of wire fence
    filled with hay

waits for the absent sheep.

A feed trough grows green algae on still water
as red berries, early-autumn-rich, straddle
    the tips of coppiced trees,
stretching unabashed towards the horizon
and the mountains, their love,
    always parted by geology and
           the glacial cut of distant ages.

A bee bolts over my head.

The hillside's slope supports my spine
as I tilt back, sweet air in my belly,

    a cabbage white's trajectory over the fence,

    men's voices from the workshops
        turning wood,

   smoothing the oak's rings
       to a glossed sheen
sculpted into new light.

High Tide
A lyric

Sail me, city, to heavens below.
Sail me, city, into depths of dark.
Sail me, city, into the hook of the estuary.
Sail me, city, to the clutch of the heart,

onto the high seas, under surfaces
through sunken shadow from old oil-lit shores
to the feline jaw of a tidal swish
and the bright-eyed bite of the cormorant.

I want the wild wet and the long depths,
strong undertow and tidal concerns,
but the harbour lights are drawing me in:
I fear dry land, sandbanks and stone.

Sail me, city, to heavens below,
Sail me, city, into depths of dark.
Sail me, city, into the hook of the estuary.
Sail me, city, to the clutch of the heart.

Onto the high sea, under surfaces
through sunken shadow from the old oil-lit shore
to the feline jaw of the tidal swish
and the bright-eyed bite of the cormorant.

O sail me, city, into the filth of the storm.
Bring the salt from my pores; let my eyes colour dawn.
O city, sail me away from settled land
into ocean's wreck and rough; back into love.

Please do not leave me earthbound.
Please do not leave me earthbound.

And the Spring Said

Open the window,
        blocked bright black
                with an oncoming darkness – night
like a fall of snow settles
        the coil of us into our homes
                and into our bodies' surrender
                      into this pebble-strewn beach of a night
washing over our small
        breaths like the moment after sex
when the day is recoiled
                and returned to where it should be –
weighting the balance of self,
                refracted and unearthed,
so it lies like a head on a sleeping chest
        and the sky whistles by like a figure
                on the road, hands in pockets
        loitering by the streetlamp
                watching Orion's belt
                      flick loose stars across the black.

St. Dynfog's Well

Water runched into the fold of the red mud banks
coils forwards through a passageway of stones
in soil, drawing its route over the edge of the brick
built pool to be held
for a while — how long?
in the flat rectangular form of the well.

I stand immersed to my neck, knees bent,
the cold lessening and the water coming on.
And facing the flow, the liquid though slow,
slides between my legs, under arms, under toes.
Do I delay its movement or hasten it?

I want to let the water pour through my bones.
Behind, the stream continues, spears
the hidden bridge by the fallen ash and over
a steep tumble to speed
a moment faster, under the church,
into the roots of the yew at the edge
of the graves and on into the village, always on.

At Gob Cave

I return from the crouched stoop of the interior,
securing my tread on the slippery broken stones

over sheep droppings, brown pearls on green grass,
to the vast valley's openness;

a funnel of cars slides into the sea and the clouds
flapping grey crepe drying in the wind –

a red tractor drives in lines below, startles the sheep.

Behind, within the cave mouth, slant-like lips needing water;
a smaller fold to the back with room for a body
to be laid out, a female head tucked onto a chest, toes
to the ceiling, stillness and dust and quietness –
quietness at the hollow of the hill,
no movement beyond down – no up and out –
        flesh to putrid onto bone
        and down down into dust.

A stopped movement and silence – still, dry space
in the crack of the rock, a deadening of sound.

*

Out here, a chestnut pony stands amongst the gorse,
lowers his head, raises grass from the roots.

The hill under me holds the handprints
of all who brought a rock to the cairn.

Like them my body wants to change dimension,
to become something other than this form.

I cannot change my bones, or fat or marrow
without dying into stillness, darkness —
my skin held in the mould of the water and remade
from dark to light, hot to cold,
all absolutes, the God, the dark, the death,
a transition: a passage between poles; points of a map.

*

At the centre of the cairn, subsidence —
a bruised head or mine shaft implosion,

wild thyme's small purple flowers,
tiny lichen yellow on grey stone, wheat grass tips.

Remember though woman, below,
always inside, under and at the centre of the hill:
she rots in the stillness of the fold,

her bones passing with time, away from their hold
to museum case or padlocked archive cupboard,

pressed into the after-life as knowledge,
pinned back together by forensic attention,

unlike now, windswept on a high hill,
my hair a struggle of snakes
blown behind the salt sea air
towards my past, laid out across the peninsula —
and my future, deep under its shores.

At Pen Môn

The stones on the beach shift like knots in a charm.
Each crunch a precursor of a spell:

    I find you inside the cairn crouched
              by the patterned stone,
                        eyeing the dark.

O Sea, I miss the blue-green heart
of your swell and fall, seal
heat immersed in your wave,
head like a coracle, nose to the cloud.

I miss each step I took along our shoreline
to the lighthouse, old quarry and cave.

Ghosts call to me from over the horizon.

I greet them as friends
as I greet the rise of the hill
and the coitus of the spring and leaf,

all of us running across the headland,

or walking the slope in a storm
or footsteps patterning
a careful tread around the silent church.

I light a candle for our passing
                      and watch it burn.

*

I carry you with me
                      each day out of the dark.

And today is about salt-traces,
the memory of darkness, of the ritual and the aftermath,
mound in the dark trees:
    an oxen burial by three entry stones.

We eat our picnic on the vantage point
and watch the rooks
    swing down, down to the copse.

And my half-immersion in your tide
                      haunts my skin;
half my shins salted and given to your wave.
The rest of me scalded by the sun
loitering somewhere
undone and fuzzy at the edges of the land.

A child hides behind
          fir trees; a young woman
lies in the long grass behind the wall.

You and me in the woods, hand in hand.
You take a picture. The hills frame the sky.

I try to write you over and over
but still I cannot say what you are.

        Woman.

You run down the lane towards the sea.
Your hands turning to skin,
waxy and folding in.

I can see you, shadow self,
shod in mud, moving across
    the stones to the beach with an ease as if
    you cannot feel them shift and
      cut beneath your soles —
rubbing smooth each corner of a future,
as you are shifting, feet to flippers
 and eyes to the horizon.
  You hear a song sung to the wind
  and peer in and under,
    until fully seal again, you bob and swim
   turning to watch three women
     picnicking on the ridge,
     watching your head perk-up,
totemic in the blue,
their open mouths calling:
Come back to us, come back.

At Sea

Darkness over the bow.
Ship on the tide
gale-freed and boxed
by salt, erosive and callow,
gnawing on the metal.

Boat battered into the storm.
You call like a nestling.
You are heard by the moon.
It blinks not unkindly
but without sensation. Your

cargo tightly packed in containers,
each component balanced in flux;
oil blobs within barrels
but remains in its limits.

The storm gathers strong arms into a gesture,
streaks you through the estuary
steered by engines' smart electronic flash
around the sandbanks towards the docks.

Batter us long waves.
Batter us wide-throated sea.
Let us find fix in the bite
of the winter wind, dark rain,
a full flush of breath,
shiny-faced and articulate.

Acknowledgements

Acknowledgements are due to the editors of the following publications, where some of this work first appeared: *Lighthouse, New Walk, Smoke, Dactyl* and *Tears in The Fence*.

'Protean Shifts' written for 'Writing on Water' at The Fordham Gallery, a barge on the Thames (in association with The Ruskin School of Art, Oxford).

'In My Ears and In My Eyes' was written for the Manchester Camarade Project, Cornerhouse Arts Centre, February 2013.

'Congleton Tapestry' was commissioned as part of 'Time to Read' for public reading at Congleton Library, 29th November 2012.

'Mossley Hill' was written for 'Mr Seel's Garden', a 'Creative Communities' AHRC participatory research project into the history of local food production in Liverpool.

'The Goat's Field' was written and presented at the Centre for Alternative Technology, Machynlleth, 8th September 2012, part of the Emergence Conference on Arts and Sustainability.

'High Tide' was first performed 18th October, 2013 by Emily Portman and the musicians of the Irish Sea Sessions, Liverpool Irish Festival, Liverpool Philharmonic Hall. The song is included on her album *Coracle* (Furrow Records, 2015).

'St. Dynfog's Well', 'At Gob Cave' & 'At Pen Mon' are from a triadic research project between illustrator Desdemona McCannon and singer Emily Portman involving song, drawing and poetry. These poems emerged from visits to St Winifrede's Well, Holywell; Gob Cave and Cairn; and Pen Môn, Ynys Môn in June/July 2014.

Acknowledgements (contd.)

With thanks to the University of Exeter and the AHRC for supporting my practice-based PhD research and thesis 'Making Connections: The Work of the Local Poet.' Special thanks also to Andy Brown and Dave Ward for editorial advice and feedback.

Riverine is the companion volume to *Blood Child* (Liverpool University Press/Pavilion, 2015).